CHINATOWN · A LEGEND OF

Old Cannery Row

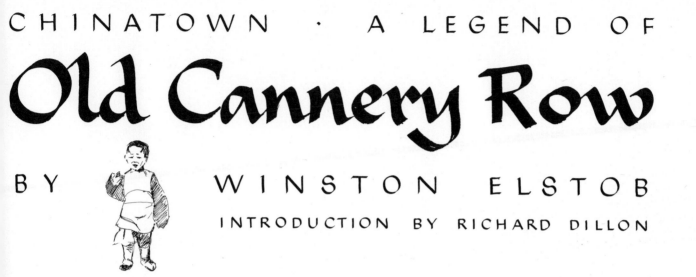

BY   WINSTON   ELSTOB

INTRODUCTION BY RICHARD DILLON

ILLUSTRATED BY JOYCE MARY ALEXANDER

Hand-lettered at The Turtle's Quill Scriptorium for the Condor's Sky Press

Condor's Sky Press

Publisher's Preface

Dorsey & Joyce Alexander walked into the Polygon bookshop on Cannery Row about one year ago and there met Winston Elstob.

Winston had a long time interest in the old Chinese community of Cannery Row. Its homes, religious edifice and boats had for decades given the Monterey shoreline a Chinese bench-mark. Shortly after the earthquake of 1906 sent San Francisco tumbling to the ground, and with the flames in San Francisco hardly quenched, other flames ended the story of the Chinatown on the bay to the south.

On their return to Berkeley, Dorsey and Joyce discussed the possibility of publishing a small hand-lettered and illustrated account of this facet of California history. We had worked together previously on the hand-lettered, illustrated book, 'Soil and Plant Analysis; A Practical Guide for the Home Gardener', published in 1964.

I feel that 'Chinatown; A Legend of Old Cannery Row' which is the result of Winston's narrative and their work justifies my agreement to publish. It is a happy privilege to publish this book to the memory of the friendly, industrious Chinese residents of Cannery Row.

by Milton Morris Weiner   at the Condor's Sky Press, Orinda, California

Introduction by Richard Dillon

In April 1853 a straggling band of a half-dozen Chinese threw their bundles and baskets on the beach at Monterey and set up camp. From their huddle of tents in the lee of Point Alones grew the fishing industry of Monterey which would, one day, make the city famous as the Sardine Capital of the world.

The humble Oriental pioneers, who had drifted south from the Mother Lode or San Francisco's 'Dupont Gai', with perhaps a brief stopover in the mines of the Coast Range, at first gathered what the Mexican-Californians called 'conchas de nacar' and the gringos termed simply 'California shell.' A larger rival group soon set up on the beach and began to take the abalone not only for its meat but for the nacre, too, and tons of shell were shipped from the old California capital. Word of the molluscy bonanza soon reached San Francisco's Chinatown and an Abalone Rush ensued.

By May 20, 1853, the San Francisco 'Daily Alta California' reported a village of some five hundred to six hundred 'Pescador Johns' on the Bay of Monterey. Before long, there were so many Chinese shacks on the (later) site of the Hopkins Marine Laboratory that Cabrillo Point became China Point, and a satellite Chinese fishing village sprang up at Pescadero Point, just west of Pebble Beach on Carmel Bay.

The Chinese did not long confine their attentions to abalone; they were soon taking all varieties of fish, oysters and mussels as well. A year after Robert Louis Stevenson's visit of 1879, David Starr Jordan, later President of Stanford University, paid the fishing port a visit as part of his survey of Pacific Coast fisheries for the Tenth United States Census. He was guided by a Portugese lad, Manuel Duarte, who shortly became a major fish dealer of the region. Jordan found the fishing craft of Monterey Bay to be of two kinds, both exotic designs. The Italians and Portugese manned lateen-rigged sloops built in San Francisco; the Chinese crewed even more bizarre craft-junks and sampans, some locally built and some constructed on San Francisco Bay by Celestial ship-wrights.

Thanks, largely, to the Cantonese pioneering the harvesting of shell, seaweed and shark oil, as well as the catching and drying of fish and abalone, Jordan found that Monterey by 1880 was second only to San Francisco as a fishing port. The Orientals used fish traps, gill nets and seines as finely meshed as mosquito bars. Although the Government Investigator neglected to list the number of junks and sampans in use off what would, one day, be Cannery Row, the settlement probably mustered a fleet of some fifteen vessels, at least, because the smaller hamlet on Pescadero Point boasted a dozen boats, itself.

There was no apparent division of labor by sex. Men and women, alike, either crewed the fishing boats or cleaned and dried the catch on shore. The unofficial Mayor of Monterey's Chinatown-on-the-Sea was the sole American citizen amongst his kith. He spoke English well and reported to Jordan that his colony shipped from two hundred to eight hundred pounds of fresh fish to San Francisco every day mainly to the mongers of

Clay Street. Doubtless the Cantonese cornered a large part of the $220,000. worth of annual profit this represented, according to Wells Fargo's records.

Almost equally important was the immense quantity of dried fish and abalone meats and shark fins sent to China from Point Alones, $12,000.-worth per month. Using every part of their catch except the traditional squeal, the Chinese created an important by product trade in abalone shell, not for pearl buttons as one might imagine, but because of a vogue – as transitory as feather boas – back East, where no mantel was complete without a souvenir of fabled California in the form of one of the nacreous shells, properly disfigured by grinding, polishing and varnishing.

By 1880 overfishing of Monterey Bay for flounder (or 'bastard halibut', as Victorians politely termed the slab-sided, pop-eyed, fish) had so reduced the catch that the Chinese were netting and drying fingerlings only two to six inches long. But the skilful Chinese continually improved their methods and ranged further afield, using set lines to secure the red rock cod which liked to lurk in the ocean depths. Two-thirds of the catch shipped to 'The City' came to be rock fish – ling cod, rock cod, blue cod or the so-called rock trout.

At first, much of the fish used to spoil on the stage trip to the rail-head at Salinas but with the completion of the railroad between Monterey and San Francisco, the latter market was assured of a continuing supply of fresh fish although demand exceeded the local, San Francisco Bay, catch.

Incredibly, that toothsome – and scarce and expensive – delicacy of 1964, abalone steak, was a drug on the market eighty to a hundred years ago. The Chinese dried the mussel, of course, for soups but the Yankees turned up their noses at the giant shellfish, except for a handful who imitated the Chinese by subjecting the steaks to long and severe cooking, also for soups. No one, apparently, even considered picking up a bludgeon to drub an abalone into the tender ambrosia it can be when properly prepared. Most gringos agreed with the sneering deprecation of the 'Daily Alta California's' editors who reported in 1853 that "the meat of the 'conchas de nacar' is esteemed as a great epicurean delicacy by all rat-eating China..."

Although Monterey's maritime Chinatown was spared by the great California earthquake of 1906, old Feng Shui (the Evil Earth Spirit) had another trick up his silken sleeve. A month later he devastated the village by fire. As is the case with all but one of the chain of Chinese fishing camps which lined California's littoral, no trace remains of Monterey's Chinese fishing village. A sole ghost vestige of the chain remains only, far to the north on Marin County's Point San Pedro – lonely, wasted China Camp.

End

CHINATOWN · A LEGEND OF

Old Cannery Row

O nce upon a time Robert Louis Stevenson, a lean, tall & gaunt figure of a man, stared out at the deep blue of Monterey Bay and listened to the haunting sounds of the surf; which he told us boomed all over the Peninsula. He, too, was entranced by the view from these shores and wrote.. "on no other coast that I know shall you enjoy, in calm sunny weather, such degrees of thunder in the sound. The very air is more than usually salt by this Homeric deep."

Stevenson paid a four month visit to Monterey, California, in 1879. He spent some of the time sick in bed with fever, but despite failing health the region cast its spell on him, as it has for countless visitors. He put down his observations, the result of many solitary walks among the pines and along the lonely beaches, in an essay entitled, "The Old Pacific Capitol".

Thus from his pen comes the following vivid description of what seem to be the first inhabitants of Cannery Row. The reader might find here and elsewhere a link with the joyful novels of John Steinbeck, when he wrote about the "Row" in terms of its bizarre characters and locale.

Stevenson happened upon a strange community tucked away

ROBERT LOUIS STEVENSON

next to the Bay and writes...

'To the east, and nearer still, you will come upon a space of open down, a hamlet, a haven among rocks, a world of surge and screaming sea gulls. Such scenes are very similar in different climates; they appear homely to the eyes of all; to me this was like a dozen places in Scotland. And yet the boats that ride in the haven are of strange outlandish design; and, if you walk into the hamlet, you will behold costumes and faces that are unfamiliar to the memory. The joss-stick burns, the opium pipe is smoked, the floors are strewn with slips of colored paper - prayers, you would say that had somehow missed their destination - and a man guiding his upright pencil from right to left across the sheet, writes home the news of Monterey to the Celestial Empire.'

And so Robert Louis Stevenson came upon the Chinese Village at the extreme northern end of Cannery Row.

2

CELESTIAL EMPIRE

In a guide book to Monterey published in 1875
we hear more about Chinatown.

'Chinatown is distant about one mile from the outskirts of town... It is admirably selected for the business carried on by its enterprising citizens - fish-curing & abalone shell shipping. Its inhabitants are frugal, industrious and well-behaved. Little or no crime occurs among them, and so far as our experience goes, they are a sober, honest set of men, and compare very favorably with their countrymen throughout the State.
The census of Chinatown is as follows :
Man Lee Company - three men and three women ;
Sun Sing Lee Company - three men, two women and one child ;
Yee Lee Company - six men, two women and three children,
and Man Sing Company - four men & one woman.'

'The Chinese industries are fishing for rockfish, cod, halibut, flounder, red and blue fish, yellowtail, mackerel, sardines and shellfish - the greater part of which are split open, salted and dried in the sun for exportation to San Francisco, whence they find their ways to the mines throughout the State and abroad. It may be estimated that the amount of

CHINATOWN 1875

4

dried fish exported from Monterey annually averages nearly one hundred tons. The Chinese also collect large quantities of abalone shells which find a ready market at twenty dollars a ton. They possess about thirty boats, nearly all of which were built by themselves. They are sailed in the Chinese fashion. Although they import from San Francisco the greater portion of their merchandise they purchase very liberally of the merchants in town, and as their trade is always for cash they are very desirable customers in these hard times.'

These accounts written about the Chinese nearly a hundred years ago do not tell the whole story. China Point, as it was and still is called, was a place of deep mystery for many of the townsfolk who, for the most part, treated its inhabitants as an unwanted and alien people. One newspaper account of the time would have you believe the Chinese were nothing less than savages living in the most degrading filth and moral depravity.

Fortunately there are many charming stories about Chinatown. Old-timers recall some unforgettable characters, black-pajama-clad and pig-tailed, padding back and forth with their peculiar jogging step. They will tell you that the village consisted of but one street, with the opening somewhere near the present location of Hovden's Sardine Cannery. There were Sing Lee and Hop Lee and Jim Jim – King of the Chinese he was called, who ran a laundry just below the Mammoth Stables. There were fish peddlers who trotted around town with rice baskets brimful of fish suspended from the ends of a pole, delicately balanced on their shoulders. When stopped for a purchase a peddlar somehow managed to produce from his person a cutting board with knife to clean the fish for you. A tin horn was slung from his shoulders on which he blared forth his presence in the neighborhood.

The village itself was an untidy jumble of unpainted shacks festooned with poles and lines hung with fish in various stages of drying. Those with weak noses would not stay very long! Nearby were fields used by the Chinese to dry squid,

5

FISH PEDDLERS

which was spread out and turned over with ordinary garden rakes. It was later put in matting bags for export to China, where it was used as a rich fertilizer for the rice fields.

Another description of Chinatown, 'Picturesque California - The Rocky Mountains and Pacific Slopes', written about 1888 and edited by John Muir, gives a down-to-earth picture of the quaint little fishing village:

'The place consists of a double row of shanties built directly on the rocky shore where here permits good-sized fishing boats to come to anchor at the owner's back door. Everything is unspeakably dirty and redolent with the odor of decaying fish. Swarthy women, and little children who are tanned as black as negroes by sun and wind, swarm in the squalid cabins and tumble about in the dust of the single street. On all the rocks about are arranged lattice-work frames that are covered with drying fish.'

'The long poles that adorn the fronts of most of the houses, the crazy balconies built over the water, the fluttering rags that hang from the clothesline, the queer boats with their lateen sails and the children with their yellow and red garments all give to the squalid place a certain attraction. When viewed from the water, it is said by those who have travelled in China to bear a striking resemblance to the native villages that line the Yangtze and other great rivers of the flowery kingdom.'

According to legend, every autumn at the end of the last century huge Chinese junks with their great lateen sails would arrive from the Orient and anchor off Chinatown, Cannery Row. Whether or not they passed customs is not clear. Their holds carried goods for the local

FLOWERY KINGDOM

7

Chinese, and they would load up with dried squid and return directly to China.

There is also the legend of the Chinese visiting California long before the Spaniards settled here in 1770. Ancient Chinese history, according to one story, records the writings of a Buddhist priest who was a great traveller and lived about 400 A.D. In one account the priest tells of a trip he made to the kingdom of Fusang, and the directions he gave would locate Fusang at about the same place as California.

But as far as our story goes there seems to be very little doubt that the Chinese were among the first to inhabit Cannery Row. If the village resembled one on the Yangtze River, this is not surprising either. Wherever the Chinese settled in California they became a little China; self-contained settlements preserving all the customs and habits of the Celestial Empire.

8

ANCIENT CHINESE LEGEND

Despite the nearby religious community of Pacific Grove with its curious blue laws and rigid moral codes, Chinatown boasted an opium den openly operated for all to see. One of the shacks included a room with tiers of bunks placed with their headboards to the wall. The smokers, usually two to a bunk, hovered over an oil lamp which heated the nodules of opium impaled on the end of a hairpin. When this became silver-colored, they rolled it onto the rims of their long-stemmed pipes, taking long, deep breaths of the stuff until their eyes glowed with satisfaction. After a while they would be stretched out in a death-like sleep with their bodies contorted in weird shapes. A phial or jar of the drug was readily available for the modest sum of ten cents, and the habit was indulged with no restraint from the local authorities.

The Joss House, always an essential part of Chinese life, could also be found on this single street of fishermen's shanties. The almost daily use of the premises with its burning incense, shelves of images, much ornate carving and historic tableaux in red and green paint, was proof enough of how important it was in their everyday life.

OPIUM DEN

'Pacific Grove Review' in 1888 writes about sightseers to the Chinese Fishing Village: 'Some pass by in sad wonder the heathen altars in every home, watch the idolatrous worship and note the gambling houses. This, they say, in a Christian town!'

The Chinese fisherman would burn much incense and consult his gods many times throughout the season. Usually he would enter the Joss House alone with little ceremony, and in a business-like fashion approach the oracle for an answer to his prayers. After an offering of food and drink to allay the appetite of his hungry god, he would kneel on a mat and call to him by name three times. He would then pick up two blocks of semi-oval shaped wood called Yum Yueng Suey and toss them in the air. The way the blocks fell would provide him with his answers. For example, if the blocks of wood fell in the same position, the gods were in an unfavorable mood and could not be consulted that day. But if they fell with their flatsides juxtaposed, perhaps the gods

JOSS HOUSE

would listen to his troubles and supply an answer. He would then knock his head on the floor three times and make his offering. When this was completed, he would take up a container of bamboo sticks and shake them toward the altar until one fell out. Each Joss stick had a number on it, and the temple keeper or priest had a book which provided an answer corresponding to the number on the 'Sticks of Fate' as they were called. Very little time had passed for the whole procedure, which now ended with special gilt-paper money burned in a furnace for proper conversion into the currency of the gods. This done, our Chinese fisherman was on his way armed with advice from his heathen temple, perhaps telling him about the next catch of fish, some pressing family matter or a risky venture.

The Chinese are best rembered by Montereyans for their New Year Celebration, when Chinatown became an open community full of feasts and street parades, writhing

paper dragons and firecrackers going off
in all directions. Little urchins would descend
upon the place and gorge themselves on
all the trays of food the Chinese passed out
with unstinting generosity, eager to share the
festivities with everybody. Many of the
local people looked forward to the celebration
and we even find the newspaper asking
for restraint and good manners so that the
people would not take advantage of the
Chinese hospitality.

A Mrs. J. C. Anthony of Monterey
recalls that the Chinese were greatly
imposed upon, as reported by
Monterey historian Mayo Hayes O'Donnell
in the 'Monterey Peninsula Herald',
March 19, 1952 : 'The hoggishness displayed
by the local urchins and residents of adult age,
in grabbing for oriental nuts, candies and
firecrackers offered by their hosts, must have
left a very unfavorable impression in the
latters mind of our boasted civilization!'

CHINESE NEW YEAR CELEBRATION

In 1891 the approach of Gung Hay Fat Choy (Happy New Year) kept the female population in the Chinese village busy for several weeks, as we learn from Mrs. O'Donnell's above-mentioned article. We hear how: 'a collection of old newspapers, every one that could be bought, went into the adornment of the walls of the dingy shanties. The cobwebs accumulated since the previous year were carefully swept down; new tinfoil ornaments and punk sticks were placed at the front doors, and an extra supply of punctured paper for distribution in honor of the Devil was received.' (The Devil would have difficulty getting through small holes)

'The deafening rattle of firecrackers announced to the Peninsula that the holidays were here, and with that announcement appeared 'an army of our Christian urchins eager to dine at Confucius' table, although that dignitary might never enter their minds at any other season of the year.'

Outside of the New Year Festival, local citizens did little socializing with the fishermen of Cannery Row. In fact, we hear of the cowhands

CHRISTIAN URCHINS

14

riding into town on a Saturday night ready to lassoo
themselves a 'Chink' and cut off his 'pigtail' (queue)
as a trophy. The history of California is full of many
such incidents far worse in degree of brutality
meted out, and the life of the Chinese not only
in jeopardy but his having little recourse to the law.
Eventually, of course, they won their rights as human
beings, but not before much woe and suffering.

There is much evidence of agitation against
the Chinese. For example, a public protest meeting
was held in Salinas on January 29, 1878 and
the first resolution passed by the gathering said:
'We, citizens of Monterey County, in mass meeting
assembled do hereby avow ourselves upon the side
of the white versus Chinese labor now and for all time.'

The newspaper, 'Monterey Californian', not only
endorsed these sentiments but went further by saying
that it 'joined the crusade against the saffron-colored
tribe, and will rejoice with our fellow-
laborers when our land is freed from
their blighting presence.'

QUEUES

The most colorful event of the New Year's festivities was the ring contest, which brought hundreds of Chinese from all over California to Chinatown. Special trainloads of them arrived to witness something legend says determined the ruler of the Chinese for the coming year. It was in the form of a contest among the Six Companies (the same organizations which had been formed in the early days of Chinese immigration to protect them against oppressors).

Each company would be represented at the Ring Contest by its hardiest members, to act as gladiators in a free-for-all greatly relished by the crowds of spectators jamming the small fishing community. They had come to see the melee of flying pigtails where the tradition was 'no holds barred'. The rules of the contest were simple.
The Ring Contest derived its name from a small round object about three inches in diameter, made of a light, strawlike material which was placed on the top of a huge firecracker about four inches thick and standing upright a foot high. When the bomb went off it would

RING CONTEST

hurl the ring into the air, to descend upon the
outstretched hands of the combatants and usually
end up in the dust. The wild scramble for its
possession was the spectacle everyone
had come to see.

16

When the dust had settled, the pile
of wriggling competitors would
in time produce a lone but happy victor
emerging triumphantly with the ring
clutched to his person. It was nothing
to see some unlucky combatant dragged over
the ground by his queue. Final victory went to
the company which collected the most rings
during the afternoon and it was declared
the Ruler of all the Chinese for the coming year.
The competition over, the celebrants
would begin the feast after suitable offering
had been made to their gods. Roast pig, chicken,
duckling, Chinese food and candy were
then consumed and the New Year's
celebration would come
to its close.

RULER OF ALL THE CHINESE

The Chinese fishermen were the first to take commercial advantage of the fishing grounds of Monterey Bay. People can still remember that odd procession of sampans in the early evening hours when they went fishing for squid. Mrs. Anthony, owner of the Log Cabin Wood Yard in Pacific Grove, sold wood to them, which they burned in wire rackets attached to the boat.

The fire of the pitch logs, red flames reflecting in the water, made an unforgettable and beautiful sight as the fishermen sailed off with their little craft into the night. The idea of the wood fire was to attract the fish and make them visible to the fishermen who caught them in nets.

Another way of catching fish was with the gill net. When the Chinese used this method they added little refinements which, to the casual spectator, must have been very amusing to watch. For example, after setting their nets they remained close by in their sampans, curious boats with two eyes painted on each prow. Without eyes, how could the boats see where they were going.

SAMPAN PROCESSION

When the fish approached, but hung back from the net, a fearful din would break out as the fishermen let out fierce yells and slapped the sides of their boats, making a furor that frightened the poor adversary into the net's meshes. They also drummed on the seats of the sampan with two sticks, and one fellow threw a pole into the water to have it rebound back to his hand. All in all, some strange goings-on!

The little fishing hamlet lasted until shortly after the San Francisco earthquake, when on the night of May 16, 1906 agitation for the removal of the Chinese in the months preceding this date reached its logical conclusion. Before reaching that dark night, however, it is worthwhile to recall some of the comments about Chinatown. In the 'Monterey New Era', Nov. 29, 1905, we read the headline 'Chinatown Will Cease 1. to Exist', and then :

'The announcement that the Pacific Improvement Company has notified the Chinese to vacate the

FIERCE YELLS

territory known as Chinatown is one of the best pieces of news we have heard for a long time. It not only means that an eyesore will be removed from one of the most beautiful and picturesque spots on the bayshore, but that a highly desirable tract will be opened up. For it is the intention of the Pacific Improvement Company, as quickly as the Chinese can get away which will be in about two or three months, to place the tract on the market. There are about thirty acres on the piece extending from Lighthouse Avenue to the waterfront. The Chinese will move to Pescadero on the Seventeen-Mile Drive.'

HIGHLY DESIRABLE TRACT

We read more of the same when the 'Monterey New Era' says[2] 'abolition would not only make building sites on the waterfront at the western end of New Monterey more valuable; but Chinatown itself would in time form as beautiful and desirable villa sites as can be found in America'. The paper also points out: 'The Pacific Improvement Company does not wish to be harsh with their Chinese tenants and is now merely waiting for them to cast about for another location. But it may be that it will eventually evict them with the aid of the law and sheriff of Monterey County'. [3]

VILLA SITES

The proverbial straw that broke the camel's back was an exceptionally large catch of squid the Chinese were drying in fields near Chinatown. A warm rainfall spoiled the fish and the stench was all over the Peninsula. They dumped the whole catch into the Bay, but it came back on the beaches with the next tide. The clamor from the townspeople with offended nostrils rose, and even the district attorney from Salinas was called in!

DRYING SQUID

It should come as no surprise to learn that at eight o'clock
at night on May 16, 1906 fire broke out among the
fishing shacks along the single crowded street
of Chinatown. The cause of the fire is a mystery to this day,
although there were reports of an explosion, men seen
running from a barn and of the difficulty the fire
department had in finding water!

The headline in the 'Pacific Grove Daily Review' read: [4.]
   'Picturesque Chinatown Only a Memory
      Fire Ends a Long Controversy
   Looting Adds to the Losses Sustained by the Chinese'.

The lead paragraph stated:
   'Shortly before eight o'clock on Wednesday evening
   fire broke out in a barn on the west end of Chinatown,
   which resulted in the almost total destruction
      of that much discussed piscatorial settlement'.

The 'Pacific Grove Daily Review' reported:
   'As soon as possible after discovery of the fire word
   was sent to this city and the Volunteer Fire Department at once
   responded to the call. Before they could reach the scene, however,

the flames had gained such headway that in spite of a
   most determined and obstinate effort their progress
could not be checked and by ten o'clock the destruction
was complete. Only low heaps of burning debris
   marked the site of the subject of many an artist's pencil.'

'The disaster throws practically two hundred
   Chinese on the hands of the community,
   not including about fifty refugees from the
San Francisco Fire who were being sheltered in
         Chinatown by their compatriots.'

'The origin of the fire is still a matter for surmise.'
'... another story is to the effect that some parties unknown
to the Chinese set the fire in the barn with incendiary intent.'

'... as a glorious and fearful spectacle this fire holds the
   record for the vicinity' the editor writes and continues:
'In contrast to the determined and heroic worth
of the firefighters one feature stands out in shameful relief
— the looting indulged in by men and boys during the
   progress of the fire. Stores and dwellings were entered
   in the confusion and articles of all kinds freely taken.

PARTIES   UNKNOWN

Some things were stolen even after they had been removed to a supposedly safe place.'

The burning of Chinatown is remembered by a resident of present day Pacific Grove, although not an eyewitness to the fire herself. She was attending the Commencement exercises that night at the Pacific Grove High School, and watching her older brother graduate.

She relates that the 9th. Cavalry, a Negro regiment camped nearby, with stables just across Central Avenue near the Work Lumber Mill, was called out to help fight the blazing flames that devoured the rickety fishing shacks of Chinatown. She remembers the troopers as being expert wranglers who broke in wild horses shipped from Wyoming and Arizona, and observes that, '...there was less trouble with the negro troops than with the infantry stationed at the Presidio'.

By all accounts the wranglers' attempt to put out the raging inferno, with little or no water available, was a gallant one. She vividly recalls seeing a burnt hole in the cap of one of their white officers, Lt. Sam B. Pierson, a friend of the family who called on them the next day.

Her father, C. K. Tuttle, she proudly recalls, was well liked by the Chinese community. He had helped them in their battle against deportation; a controversy we have noticed that was carried on through the years by a certain section of the citizenry who wished to see the Chinese removed from California.

THE RAGING INFERNO

24

From the 'Monterey New Era', weekly, May 23, 1906:

'The firemen of Pacific Grove and the members of the New Monterey Hose Co. turned out when the alarm was given and made strong efforts to stay the flames. Their efforts were ineffectual because the only water available was a single small stream played through a garden hose.'

The Monterey Peninsula Herald, March 25, 1941, quotes an interview with a local cigar store owner, Mr. Bill Sorensen, which appeared in the Pacific Grove Daily Review, May 17, 1906:

'When the fire started, it just kept going until Chinatown was destroyed. For days afterwards, there was gossip about it that the Pacific Improvement Company, the superholding company of California's 'Big Four', had started the fire themselves.'

Eyewitnesses say no Chinese were to be found around the place. They had fled to Point Joe abandoning all their possessions. Losses were estimated at about twenty-five thousand dollars. We hear of a collection being made on the Chinese behalf a couple of days later in Monterey when twenty-seven dollars was raised.

The 'New Era' added one last touch:

'Now that the settlement is so nearly destroyed they will not be allowed to rebuild.'

TWENTY SEVEN DOLLARS

When they did come back, the authorities were waiting with a thirty-six page eviction notice which was the real end of Chinatown.

26

The Chinese never settled as a fishing village again and scattered to different parts of the County. There were, however, a few families left who moved back and formed a small colony at the northern end of Cannery Row. When the canneries came along, almost all of the earlier workers were Chinese, and the tradition of using Chinese exclusively lasted until the early nineteen-thirties.

End

Notes

1. This information was in a supplement insert in that issue.

2. The date of the issue quoted is May 14, 1902 (4 years before the fire).

3. The date of the issue quoted is February 14, 1906.

4. This quotation is reprinted in the Monterey Peninsula Herald,
   March 25, 1941.

The author and The Turtle's Quill scriptorium wish to acknowledge
the kind and helpful cooperation of staff members of the following
institutions.

Bancroft Library
Monterey Public Library & Pacific Grove Public Library
San Francisco Maritime Museum
California Historical Society

The Turtle's Quill

SCRIPTORIUM

2571 SHATTUCK AVE., BERKELEY, CALIFORNIA

This book was entirely 'written out' by hand by Dorsey Alexander.
It was illustrated with wash drawings by Joyce Alexander

1965

∴